Arizen Treasure

CHANTAI FINESSE

adash of finesse
& CO.

Copyright © 2018 Chantai Finesse

Published by **A Dash of Finesse & Co.**

All rights reserved. This book or any portion thereof may not be reproduced, stored in a retrieval system, or transmitted in any form or by any means, electronic, mechanical, photocopying, recording, or otherwise, without the express written permission of the copyright owner except for the use of brief quotations in a book review.

This book is sold subject to the condition that it shall not, by way of trade or otherwise, be lent, resold, hired out, or otherwise circulated without the publisher's prior consent in any form of binding or cover other than that in which it is published and without a similar condition including this condition being imposed on the subsequent purchaser. Under no circumstances may any part of this book be photocopied for resale.

The events an people depicted in the story are told to the best of Chantai Finesse's memory and based entirely on her perspective. The author and publisher do not assume and hereby disclaim any liability to any party for any loss, damage or disruption caused by errors or omissions, whether such errors or omissions result from negligence, accident, or any other cause.

For any information regarding permission contact
Chantai Finesse via **hello@dashoffinesse.com**

Copy Edited by **Kim-Lee Patterson**
Design by **Euan Monaghan**

Printed in the United States of America
First Publication, 2018

Paperback ISBN: 978-1-7752055-1-7
eBook ISBN: 978-1-7752055-0-0

dashoffinesse.com

Acknowledgements

A book of this nature could not have been possible had it not been for the consult, encouragement and assistance of others:

- My family, Richie, Zariyah, Xzekiyel, Tziona and Kelilah who supported my writing through the entire process and encouraged me to keep going
- My mother and father who contributed to the process and helped me find closure in various aspects of my life as I penned this story
- My sister, Junille and Rivkah who were both the sounding boards I needed and helped me reflect and gain insight into the experiences we faced growing up
- Nats, Vana and Srijita who took the time to read through

what I had at various points and encourage me to bring my story to life

- Aunt Maureen and Aunt Vin for encouraging me to always follow my passions
- Belinda "Kamshuka" Photography, Shani (Captured By Shani), Kenneth Sookhai (WksbyKS) for the phenomenal photography featured throughout
- Makini Smith, Kike-Lola Odusanya, Kim-Lee Patterson, Euan Monaghan, Kamar Martin, Faces By Pureness for all the technical and creative support to bring this book to fruition

Dedication

This book is certainly a first of firsts for me. I am truly filled with gratitude to God and deeply honoured that despite the way my journey began, it was all meant to be in order for my life to be as fulfilling as it is today!

Zariyah, before you were born, although I felt a deep sense of purpose for my life, it was not yet realized and I could have never imagined the direction and shape it would take after having you!

You are an amazing child, full of great promise and such love. Your tender spirit refreshes me today and every day from the moment you entered the world and into my life! You have such quiet confidence, never feeling the need to flaunt it and I am certain that when you allow that gift to be directed outside of your comfort, you will truly be amazed to see what awaits you! You are my gift from God

Himself. My princess, treasured and adorned by Him – Zariyah Adaya

Love you always,

Mummy

_____

(Be a part of this journey and place your name here)

When my passions for reading, writing and doodling collided together, they created this particular format to share my story. My goal was to create a book in such a way that incorporates your own story relating to where you presently are, and allows you the space to jot down notes, highlight things and use the posed questions as reflections for yourself while you continue to explore this journey of life with me.

Each chapter has a "*SELAH*" moment meaning to "*Pause and Reflect*" where you can take a moment to see how each chapter relates to something you may have experienced for yourself.

The "*THOUGHTS – NOTES – DOODLES*" section is literally a free for all. Whether you are more expressive through writing, cutting and pasting inspirational objects or drawing something that derives from your imagination, this is your blank canvas to do whatever you want.

My reason for laying this out in this manner goes back to a genuine belief that I have. Every story matters. There's a lesson to be learned by every story you hear and there is also a story to share that only you can tell. You have enough substance and worth within you that deserves a platform to be poured out…and even if not today, or maybe not tomorrow, definitely while there is breath in your body. One day you may look back to what you added here and it will be the jump off point for undertaking an opportunity, perhaps even to share your own story.

Thank you in advance for imparting your story alongside mine! Together we can literally move mountains!

Sincerely yours,

Chantai Finesse

Table of Contents

Acknowledgments 3

Dedication 5

Introduction 7

Preface 11

One – Foundation 15

    Pause & Reflect (selah) 33

    Thoughts – Notes – Doodles 35

Two – Growing Pains 37

    Pause & Reflect (selah) 55

    Thoughts – Notes – Doodles 57

Three – Honest Admission 59

    Pause & Reflect (selah) 73

    Thoughts – Notes – Doodles 77

Four – Brokenness 79

    Pause & Reflect (selah) 95

    Thoughts – Notes – Doodles 97

Five – Transition 99

    Pause & Reflect (selah) 115

    Thoughts – Notes – Doodles.. 117

Six – Zariyah 119

    Pause & Reflect (selah) 131

    Thoughts – Notes – Doodles 133

Seven – Treasured 135

    Declaration 141

    Thoughts – Notes – Doodles 147

Preface

You don't wake up one day and suddenly find yourself transformed into a heroine. And unless you're a part of some production, you don't randomly discover having superhuman powers either! Don't get me wrong, heroes do exist—but, it takes growth, and a whole lot of it—integrating with the physical, mental, emotional and especially the spiritual aspects of a person to get there. The process cannot be rushed, blueprinted, or followed like a recipe, because the path leading there is unique to each person. And the standard by which one measures themselves as a heroine? Equally as unique. Oftentimes, she is unaware that each action she took would cause her to become recognized.

Oxford Dictionary defines a heroine as "a woman admired or idealized for her courage, outstanding achievements, or noble qualities." We can examine our pasts and acknowledge the women who fought to be treated as equal to their male counterparts. We can reflect on those who sought to overcome discrimination based on their age, race, cultural practices, or faith. We can explore even further and see how many women we see every day, living next door, working with us. We buy from them, we listen to them, and despite them not wearing capes or masks, they stand apart from others and aid in the continued growth of our society—pushing barriers that once stifled those considered "less than."

Have the gears in your mind started moving yet?

It doesn't take a particular type of woman, with specific genetics or health to be a woman society admires. You simply must understand that you've already started on that journey, long before you may have realized it.

> *[11] For I know the thoughts that I think toward you, says the* L*ORD*, *thoughts of peace and not of evil, to give you a future and a hope. [12] Then you will call upon Me and go and pray to Me, and I will listen to you. [13] And you will seek Me and find Me, when you search for Me with all your heart. [14] I will be found by you, says the* L*ORD*, *and I will bring you back from your captivity; I will gather you from all the nations and*

Preface

from all the places where I have driven you, says the L<small>ORD</small>, and I will bring you to the place from which I cause you to be carried away captive. (Jeremiah 29:11-14 NKJV)

One — The Foundation

My childhood wasn't unlike most, I'd suppose. A native of England, I was born to Jamaican parents, and we all immigrated to Canada when I was three years old. A year later, my sister was born. During my adolescence, we spent what would be our longest period of stability in the quaint town of Castleton, ON. We lived in what I would later realize was a generously-sized home on a hill, overlooking an extraordinary view of our 18 acres of land. Nature surrounded us. You could feel how fresh the air was as it filled your lungs, and the view consisted of deer and other wildlife roaming the grounds during the day. The night sky was so clear you could see the stars illuminate their constellations. We often spotted wolves prowling about in their packs at night.

It was a life of simplicity. The world around us contrasted

greatly with what we saw on television and perceived as reality. We were not raised to be flashy, due in part to my mother. She emphasized modesty and so I didn't realize that we lived quite well. I had great friends growing up, some of whom had horses. Others were from families that ran farms. They showed me unconditional care and respect, which I have always remembered them for. Their encouragement carried me through the difficulties I faced being the only visible minority in the school, until my sister joined me four years later.

Though I loved my friends and usually felt like one of the group, every time I caught a glimpse of my reflection in a mirror or window, I engaged in a battle of the mind—questioning my value, my likability, and whether I really had the approval of those around me. I faced my share of ignorant comments and finger pointing, which often left me wondering why I was so different from everyone around me. In hindsight, perhaps that's when the people-pleasing nature took root. I strove to work hard, stay out of trouble, and get good grades—in hopes of going under everyone's radar. However, rather than blending in, I was recognized instead. During the last full school year I spent at Castleton P.S., I achieved recognition for being "Most Creative Writer" and the "Hardest Working Student" in my class, not to mention representing my

One — The Foundation

school when I was placed in Northumberland's track and field meet for 100 and 200m.

Although I tried to suppress my authentic self, the truth that lives within can never be completely subdued, no matter how much one tries. I hated being the odd one out among the people around me, but when I was in my own company or in the comfort of my immediate family, those very qualities that made me, me, were things I loved. I was the girl who loved researching black history, exploring the accomplishments and hardships of the people I descended from. I watched programing that focused on cultural lifestyle and trends, just so I could figure out who—or what—I was supposed to be. I spent hours in headphones. I listened to vinyls and CDs varying in genre from R&B to Rock, Jazz, Funk, Hip Hop and everything in between … I took it all in!

As a professional bass guitarist, my father mainly played in two UK bands, Intrigue, and Black Stallion while living in London. Here, in Canada, he turned one of our garages into a recording studio, naming it Chantaija after my sister and me. He and four other men created the rock band, Potentially Dangerous. I took any chance I could to sit in the control room, with the reel to reels—absorbing all the senses that the music would awaken. I loved the power of sound and music way back then, and still do to this very day! When I wasn't engaged in music, I was reading or writing. Reading became my escape. Fully submersing myself into any book, I'd think of myself as the protagonist, imagining what my life would be, had I been born in another place or era. From suspense, to drama, and from teenage fiction to civil rights' recounts, I used what I learned to create novels of my own, especially when I didn't like the ending to a story I read. I had no shortage of imagination to draw from. My sister and I often made up stories when we played with our toys. I recall the many adventures we would create. We even made props to go with them, to represent things we didn't actually have. Once, we made a wheelchair out of krazygears for a doll whose legs broke off.

I spent most of my childhood living in a bubble, daydreaming. I longed for a life different from the one I had, one where I could make a difference in people's lives, inspiring them to have the courage to do great things. I wanted to give others a sense of purpose in their lives, just as Nelson Mandela, Martin Luther King Jr, Malcolm X, or even Barak and Michelle Obama have done for so many others. Instead, my reality fell flat. I suffocated within myself, trapped in a cocoon where my limited presence stifled and bound my aspirations.

One — The Foundation

I felt like I could do nothing about my present state, being too young and lacking the je ne sais quoi to be like them in the near future.

By the time I was twelve, hardship uprooted us from our family home. We ended up staying with friends of my mother in Ajax, ON. Finally injected into surroundings with more diversity, I was both excited and nervous to start this new chapter. But it proved to be more challenging than I expected. Again, I stood out! Not just from those different from me, but from people within my own culture. Could I catch a break, for once?! Deflated, I resigned myself to thinking that I was not meant to fit in anywhere. I'd be a misfit no matter where I went! The positive in all this was that I was able to befriend classmates diverse from myself. Learning about their cultures and practices opened up an entire world of understanding to me. But, apart from that, being an awkward preteen trying to assimilate was just not working in my favour.

We spent that summer vacation in Chicago, IL, after which I felt more confident and ready to tackle grade seven. Upon our arrival back home, my sister and I were taken aback to learn that our parents were divorcing, and we'd be moving elsewhere. The divorce wasn't much of a surprise. Finding our new accommodations to be a single bedroom in a women's shelter with only a bunkbed as furniture was. That opened the floodgates of my oppressed tears.

In the early stages, some attempt was made to maintain a sense of normalcy in our new situation. We were kept enrolled in the school we attended the year before, but now we had to wake up an hour earlier to catch the "GO" from Oshawa, ON to Ajax, then trek from the bus stop to my mother's friend's house and go to school from there. After school, we didn't have the luxury of leisure time to talk or hang out with friends as we rushed to catch the bus home. That's probably when the rebellion started to creep in. I'd purposely miss the bus, so I could walk to the plaza with my friends, gaining one more hour of what I thought was reasonable to have something of a normal teenage life. This new habit didn't go over well with my mum. Two weeks later, we were enrolled in the local elementary school a short distance from the shelter.

As if adjusting to yet another school in the middle of the schoolyear wasn't difficult enough, imagine how I felt when the popular students happened to hang out by the cafeteria window of the shelter and spotted me in there? Mortified, to say the least, and even less enthusiastic to face them the next day at school. Surprisingly though, I found out that I wasn't the only one in an unfortunate situation. I came to learn about the ugly side of my rose-coloured

One — The Foundation

outlook on the world. Some of the friends I made in Oshawa came from environments of all kinds: abuse, molestation, violence, and alcoholism. They were used to seeing new kids at school who came and left the same shelter I now lived in. After a short while, things began to look up. Eventually, we were moved into a different wing of the shelter where we had our own separate apartment. It was nice to finally have our own space, not sharing a bathroom with countless others. We could choose what to eat, rather than settle on the cafeteria's menu for breakfast, lunch and dinner.

Unfortunately, the mounting stress proved to be too severe for my hard-pressed mother. She spent a lot of time in bed, and soon I learned that she would have to go to the hospital for some time over the winter holidays. My father returned to Canada for good after working abroad, and so we started visiting him regularly on the weekends. Once this new dilemma arose, arrangements were made for us to stay with him. So went yet another change in a short span of time, leading me to conclude that my mother's choices had led to us experiencing such an unstable life. Now, I had an opportunity to change those circumstances for the better! I always viewed my father as the pillar of strength and stability within our family. When he wasn't around, my mother's stress levels were apparent. She never had time for us, always busy with everything else it seemed. But, my father? He was always so easy going. If I only knew then what I know now about the stresses of living as a single parent, and striving to do right by your children with limited assistance!

I was twelve when, with my "vast amounts of reasoning," I packed my sister's and my belongings in suitcases, trekking across the way to find our father when the time came to go through with the arrangement for the holidays. He and his "friend" T were startled at the amount of luggage we brought with us.

I laid out the plan to both adults, explaining the benefits of changing residence. Pointing out the impact it would have on our health, growth, and overall progress, I also thought that it would be good for my mother to have a chance to sort herself out, so she could be the mother we needed her to be. I read a lot back then, books that portrayed varying fictional relationships. It was with that knowledge that I gauged how real life should play out. My speech worked, and when school resumed after winter break, my sister and I started our third school that academic year in yet another city, Scarborough, ON. For me, it was the start to a new beginning with only positivity to gain.

And, I was right. Rouge Valley was a fairly new school and overall, the students came from good homes. I made friends easily

One — The Foundation

and felt like I could finally put down stable roots. In all my various moves, I learned the art of adaptation, showing only the layers of myself that were relevant to whatever situation I was in. My circumstances taught me how to wear masks. The wholesome image that appeared to transcend among these students caused me to hide any details of my past that didn't fit the narrative of my current scenario. But, a lot still went on behind the scenes.

Conflicts arose when my mother came out of the hospital, ready to take us back. I was not willing to return. My sister was too young to understand what was happening, and the chaos that made us (mostly me) public enemy #1 in the eyes of all those close to my mother. I took to lying to cover up the internal struggle. Fighting feelings of rejection, guilt, and depression as following our change of primary caregiver, I also had to cope with multiple suicide attempts by my mother. Any time we visited her friends, judgment and anger ensued. All this—while trying my best to conform to the new family dynamic consisting of my father and new mother figure. My mother ended up going away for a time to recoup. In her absence, I settled into a new life with my father, sister and T, who requested that we start calling her mom. As a Christian, she started to regularly attend church, so we followed suit.

This church was lively with a large population of involved

youth. That was the first time I remember actually wanting to attend services each week. I still remember attending service to ring in the New Year at that church. When the call was made to come to the altar, it felt like the right thing to do. I wanted so badly to live as freely as the other youth in attendance seemed to, but after walking away, I felt no differently. My personal revelation of salvation wouldn't come until weeks later, when I took another girl with me who wanted prayer, but didn't want to go alone. I'm not sure how her experience turned out, but my life has not been the same since I left that altar!

> *³ Praise be to the God and Father of our Lord Jesus Christ! In his great mercy he has given us new birth into a living hope through the resurrection of Jesus Christ from the dead, ⁴ and into an inheritance that can never perish, spoil or fade. This inheritance is kept in heaven for you, ⁵ who through faith are shielded by God's power until the coming of the salvation that is ready to be revealed in the last time. ⁶ In all this you greatly rejoice, though now for a little while you may have had to suffer grief in all kinds of trials. ⁷ These have come so that the proven genuineness of your faith—of greater worth than gold, which perishes even though refined by fire—may*

One — The Foundation

result in praise, glory and honor when Jesus Christ is revealed. ⁸ Though you have not seen him, you love him; and even though you do not see him now, you believe in him and are filled with an inexpressible and glorious joy, ⁹ for you are receiving the end result of your faith, the salvation of your souls. (1 Peter 1:3-9 NIV)

Looking for a sense of normalcy and acceptance as a young teen, I eagerly obliged. Back then, I viewed my mother as weak, so I overwrote her existence with my stepmother's. To me, my mum was a woman who was too overwhelmed by life, and who ended up hurting the daughter she was supposed to love, when her back was against the wall. I grew calloused towards her, pinning her up as example of who I never wanted to be—unhappy and uncaring towards herself, which made her seem incapable of showing love to others. It wasn't until much later in life that our relationship would gradually heal, as I matured and came to understand her position.

When my father and stepmother married, they decided to move to Mississauga, ON--three weeks after starting my freshman year of high school with my Rouge Valley friends. Blindsided and thrown out of my comfort zone, I discovered I would be attending a Catholic high school, and decked out in an unflattering, green uniform. I spent the Thanksgiving weekend catching up on my classes, as I was three weeks behind. I mostly kept to myself, but did manage to make a few friends. Over the two and a half years that I attended that school, I struggled with my identity. The influence of the negative associations I had at the time did not help.

When I started grade eleven, I was completely out of my element. No longer doing well in my studies, I lost much of the passion I use to have for school. I was always late for classes, doing the minimum to get by. The breaking point came after a conversation with the Vice Principal. She stated that I'd end up like the other individuals who spent most of their days in her office—with no ambition and no hope of a real future. I wasn't a troublemaker; I was simply unmotivated. That was enough for my father to declare in a meeting with her that followed that he would authorize my immediate withdrawal from the school, as I would not need any of their assistance to make it in life!

That was it!

Just like that, at seventeen years old, I became a high school dropout—with parental consent! Trying to reason with me, my mother contacted her relatives in England and an intervention was staged. I was to go over and stay with them. Not much was achieved during that mini-vacay. However, with a change in heart, my father

One — The Foundation

and stepmother called to advise that our trip would be cut short. I'd be enrolled into a new school that September. So, I only ended up missing a semester.

Upon landing back in Canada, we barely began to unpack our luggage before discovering that we'd be moving, yet again. This time we were relocating from Mississauga to Milton, ON—after a short stint in Richmond Hill, ON.

Yes, I can probably guess what you're thinking right now!

After settling in at Milton District H.S, I became more involved, even joining the basketball team. If you knew me then, you'd understand that the only basketball skill I had was looking like someone who played, as far as the school was concerned anyway. I must admit, I did look good in that Mustang uniform, big afro and all. And I did have some minor defensive skills. Still—it was nice to be part of something! Aside from my new extracurricular activity, being yet another minority in a highly undiversified school, I made it a point to raise awareness of inclusion. I wrote a letter and met with my teachers and principal to address my concerns about the intolerance I saw in the students' display. That was probably when I first demonstrated my passion for speaking up against injustice and the ignorance I saw around me.

While at Milton District, I formed and solidified a friendship with a girl nicknamed "Chylds." It was reminiscent of what I had with my Rouge Valley friends. She was a Scarborough native, and also had her fair share of interesting life experiences. It was nice to befriend someone who could understand my point of view. We respected each other's differences and celebrated our similarities. She helped me get through a lot!

The next semester, however, we moved again—this time, northeast, to Brampton, ON. Life was thrown up in the air again, and I struggled to assimilate with my new surroundings. After completing that schoolyear, I went back for one more semester, enrolling as a co-op student so I could get away from school and everything else.

Following our move to Brampton, I would move another eight times over seven years. This is one of the many lessons I have learned:

"All roads lead here"

One — The Foundation

I may never understand why while so many people I know have been in the same home for most of their lives, I've always jumped from place to place—constantly in a state of transition.

I've concluded that, no matter the journey or the road travelled between them, it's the people we encounter, the cultures we acquire, and the experiences we gain that lead us to this very moment—where we are right now. And this will continue until our own life's journey has ended.

My experiences have taught me to **refrain from "settling"** – whether it be in a home, a job, or a goal. If I start to feel stagnant, I become restless. To compliment that, however, within the past few years I've learned the importance of being still. There are certain times when we are meant to move, but there are also moments when we need to pause.

Another word we can use instead of stillness is tranquility. **Sometimes, it is in that stillness, or state of tranquility, that we can recoup and recover from the last change, preparing us for something even bigger coming our way.** Both of these states complement each other and bring balance to our lives.

Pause & Consider = Selah

1. When you reflect on your own journey and look at where you've travelled up to this point – what comparisons can you draw between your past self and your present self?

2. What passions do you have now that were ignited from way back then?

    a. Are they still relevant to your growth, or are they holding you back?

3. Being able to share our own journeys with others can do double duty in helping them, while sometimes bringing clarity to ourselves. What are some ways you can use your journey to help others? (A loved one? A child? A neighbour? A co-worker?)

Lord, I pray for the individual reading this chapter. Reveal yourself to them; may they catch a glimpse of the greatness You have in store for them. Help them to find clarity in their own life, concerning the changes they've been through. We may never fully comprehend why the things we experience in life happen as they have, but I thank You for the promises You made, and find solace in Your word. I ask that You would do the same for this reader, as Romans 8:28 (NKJV) states:

> *28 "And we know that all things work together for good to those who love God, to those who are the called according to His purpose."*

In Your precious name we pray, Amen.

Thoughts – Notes – Doodles

Two — Growing Pains

If asked to choose one word to define me during any of the foundation-building moments of my teen years, I'd choose, "awkward."

During those developmental years, I molded my behavior to accommodate what I believed others expected me to say or do. Within myself, however, I couldn't grasp what it meant to be Chantai Finesse. Other girls seemed sure of themselves, known for their flawless physiques, and experimenting with makeup and hairstyles that made them stand out.

These things were foreign to me. Apart from an interest in nail art, I pretty much kept to silver or glittery polish, and wore my hair in a big fro or puff with the front wrapped—if it wasn't braided. Other than that, nothing distinguished me amongst my peers. I felt overlooked. I didn't fit into the cliques with straightened hair or weaves. I didn't fit with those who wore make up, either, and although I enjoyed when others saw things that they could try on me to make me look the part, for me to be able to pull off the creative concepts all on my own, meant that I would have to see past the perception I had of myself. I felt like an unattractive, short girl who wore glasses—never able to be like my peers who could walk in heels with coloured contacts and physiques that gave them ability to pull off the uniform kilts. I hated my knees so much that I donned unflattering pants and never showed my legs. The constant comparisons I made in my mind convinced me that I could never measure up.

Some of those beliefs changed, though. In grade nine, I somehow managed to attract the attention of a tall, dark, and handsome older boy. He said all the things I craved to hear from the opposite sex, and I was putty in his hands! With him, I had my first kiss and began to fantasize about a happily-ever-after. Wedding details were planned long before I could even fathom the possibilities of my own future, or even have the finances to support such a grandiose affair (like flying every relative in and renting an entire hotel to accommodate them, to say the least).

Certain things arose that I should have been more alert to. This

Two — *Growing Pains*

relationship did not mirror a healthy one. But, when you have a circle of individuals, especially within your family, who thrive on manipulation, it's difficult to be open to opinions of those with differing views. These others tried to warn me about him, but as far as I was concerned, it was prophesied (and I use this term extremely lightly given the circumstance) that we were supposed to get married. Due to this, despite major ups and downs between us, we stayed together for the better part of my teens, and into early adulthood. There was prospect surrounding his destiny for the ministry. I attempted to break things off on multiple occasions because of the uncertainties I had, and was often met with accusations of my unworthiness to him. Members of my household treated me like an outsider, subjecting me to ridicule and other punishments because of my presumed unwarranted attitude, excuses, and overall behaviour. At one point, we had broken up while he was living in my family's home. I was told to move my things into the guest bedroom while he claimed ownership of my room. It was my job to wake up every morning and ensure he had breakfast and was made lunch for work. I was to serve him first at meals, and even wash and hang his clothes at one point. I believe it was a punishment for my choosing not to continue accepting his behaviour as a boyfriend who found it amusing to verbally abuse me, drape me by my clothing, call me his b****, and cheat on me with anyone he chose—since I was not putting out. It wasn't until later, when I disclosed to my father that I had locked myself in a bathroom to escape from him when we broke up for the final time that, at the next sign of trouble, my father told him to move out. My stepmother had made me promise not to tell anyone about the anger my ex displayed in her presence during that incident. It frightened her to the point of telling me to run while she tried to calm him down. Still, he unlocked the bathroom door where I was hiding and dared me to say or do something if I was brave enough to see what his response would be. I barely breathed.

After he left the bathroom, I went down to the basement, contemplating what to do next. When he came downstairs and found me, all I could think of saying was that I was sorry. He told me that if I was, I needed to get down on my knees and beg, to show him I was truly remorseful. When I replay that moment back in my head, fearful as I was, the image that kept playing in my mind while his words echoed in the background was of a dog obeying its master's command.

I don't recall whether I was so lost in my thoughts that he decided to go back upstairs, but I do remember that—as low and as worthless he lead me to believe I was, I knew I in no way resembled anything that should be treated so inhumanely. It was then that it

Two — Growing Pains

dawned on me that I was free of the stronghold that compelled me to keep silent for so long. I used to shut up the second he looked at me a certain way. I thought his behavior was permissible—warranted, even. I thought it was my place as a woman, and that my position was lower than it really was.

I wasn't the only one at home going through difficulty. It often felt like everyone in the house (a minimum of eight members at any given time) was against me, due to the constant shifting of blame. If someone in the house was targeted for an offence, everyone else typically kept quiet to avoid negative attention being drawn to them—whether they agreed with the treatment or not. I often felt targeted, and it did not help that my upbringing with my father and stepmother was one of male dominance. This mentality made for a disastrous recipe, especially with the boys and young men who would come to our house, lacking a full sense of their own identity or having positive male role models in their own lives. Even though our family consisted of the two parents, my sister, and I, we adopted various members over the years. They frequently mentored youth who were considered in need of more attention than my sister and I apparently were. Due to this, any male who was brought in automatically had more rights than us and any other females in the house—especially in the absence of my parents. We were not allowed to do anything without their consent. As I've mentioned, we were trained to get up before the guys woke up to make their lunches and we did the cleaning and the bulk of the housework. We also prepared meals after returning home from services, while everyone else relaxed. This was meant to prepare us for our roles as subservient wives. It isn't that learning any of these skills was wrong—but the context in which they were taught was. We shouldn't have been raised to believe that being maids or servants with fewer rights was equivalent to being the help-mate or virtuous woman God created us to be.

> [18] *And the LORD God said, "It is not good that man should be alone; I will make him a helper comparable to him."*
> [22] *Then the rib which the Lord God had taken from man He made into a woman, and He brought her to the man.*
> [23] *And Adam said:*
> *"This is now bone of my bones*
> *And flesh of my flesh*
> *She shall be called Woman,*
> *Because she was taken out of Man." (Genesis 2:18, 22-23 NKJV)*

Nothing in the description above denotes women as inferior beings. Women were created "comparable" to their male counterparts, and

Two — Growing Pains

rather than being taken from a body part in front or behind, above or below, God used a rib taken from the side of the man to create women. It's the combination of both individuals, building each other up, that creates a powerful family dynamic. I had to start over by removing the negative assumptions I carried about a woman's place. Not only did I have to realize my own worth from within, but I also had to carry that belief in the behaviour that I allowed others to display towards me. This is a constant struggle for women, who are confronted by individuals who challenge these beliefs every single day.

Even though I was completely out of my element when I broke up with the man I had basically grown up with, I realized that the hardest part was already done! I could now work to envision my life with someone who would treasure and value me in the way I was meant to be from the beginning. My next relationship showed me that there were men with the capacity to be strong in their ability to love, while still having self-worth. However, with our spiritual beliefs not being on par, I still felt a lack and while taking a mutual break from our relationship, I realized that God still had more for me. That became evident when the same guy called one day to tell me that he had gotten another girl pregnant, but was so sorry for hurting me.

As a side note, for any men who may be reading this: NEVER tell a girl that she deserves better after you admit or get caught doing something wrong. We already know it….even if it's way deep down inside, and we don't want to admit it to ourselves. You saying it feels like you're rubbing in the fact that we haven't reached our happily-ever-after as yet, which we clearly know just from you admitting that you're not the end goal.

And so, the growth continued into my twenties…and all the pains along with it!

Walking through Square One on my way home after work, a man approached me. He said he had seen me before and wanted to say something then, but missed his opportunity. So, this time, he made it a point to ensure we spoke. He got my attention. We exchanged numbers, had some promising conversations, and ultimately made plans to meet up. When we did, we took a romantic stroll. He offered me his jacket. The stars twinkled. It was all so amazing! I swear the scene was taken right out of a movie full of romantic indulgence and tears of happiness somewhere in the script.

Another date was set. This time, I was to meet him at his home. I was wowed. He had his own place? Independent, and looking to get serious? I figured with the gentlemanly behaviour he showed me, and the amazing conversations we had to date, this showed progress.

Two — Growing Pains

Could I have finally found the one?

What I left with that day was absolute confusion, my mind reeled with many thoughts and one major question….Does it matter?

Is the time, place, culture, colour, religion, state of mind, or the state of health relevant when a crime is committed against a person?

Is it?

I knew him, though someone I met pretty recently. I believed we pursued the same goals. I was at his house. I wasn't drunk, not under any kind of influence, and therefore in a clear state of mind. Because of these facts, I ran from the truth. If the above was all true, and I were to tell someone, then obviously, I was to blame for everything that happened. It was my fault. And if it was my fault, then it couldn't….and wouldn't… be considered rape, right?

Before that day, I had a perception of what types of girls become sexual assault victims. You hear the comments. You see the fingers wagging in disapproval as a scantily clad female walks by. Why? Well, she's "asking" for trouble. Problem was, I wasn't that girl. I was the one who said her prayers before going to sleep, studied her Bible, and even lead Bible studies at home and a few for the youth group I had attended. We held family prayer meetings, and I wasn't even allowed to attend school dances. I came from a broken home under rehabilitation and—despite the unbalanced gender roles—my father and stepmother did try to encourage a God-centered home.

I wasn't a "bad" girl.

Looking back now, I see that my perception of bad was skewed. A person who behaves badly is often the product of an experience that went unaddressed or unresolved, whether the individual refuses to, or simply does not know how to go about finding resolution. I became one of those people. After my experience, the weight that pressed down on me caused any respect I initially had for myself to disappear. I was in a lesser place than when I was with my high school boyfriend, and ignoring the situation left me unable to look myself in the eye when in front of the mirror. I knew from that moment that my life would be altered forever, but where my thoughts tuned in to the negative glass-empty type of perception, God would slowly, over time, reveal the complete opposite!

As a teenager taking part in youth groups in more than a few congregations, I remember the countless teachings I heard from ministers. I remember the prayers by elders, lectures from my and others' parents on the sacredness of our bodies. They would often recite from the same following passage:

[19] *"Or do you not know that your body is the temple of the*

Two — Growing Pains

Holy Spirit who is in you, whom you have from God, and you are not your own? [20] *For you were bought at a price; therefore glorify God in your body and in your spirit, which are God's." (1 Corinthians 6:19-20 NKJV)*

The Word of God isn't the piecing together of a bunch of random thoughts. Everything written in the Bible is purposefully placed to connect perfectly for each person who needs to hear and take away from its teachings. Now as I reflect on this oft-cited passage, the part that resonates with me most is, "...and you are not your own..."

I mean, honestly—I've learned lessons while I was younger that taught me that I could or could not do certain things. But, after growing up and developing my own convictions, some of those things no longer ring true, and are not exercised in my life any longer. However, where it comes to engaging sexual activities, whether I decide to ignore the "internal nagging" or come up with excuses for why my actions are permissible, I know that I'm doing something wrong. If my body *is* in fact my own, then why do I feel conflicted when I am making a decision that only affects it... me? The only answer I could find is that God reiterates through His Spirit dwelling in us, and that my body—the one He loves and breathed life into—is an extension of His. This can be viewed in the same way a child's actions, though made to affect only themselves, whether good or bad, will still impact their parents who love them. God sees our bodies, the very essence of our being, as important; priceless, invaluable, precious, and essential. It doesn't only describe how God views us, but how we ought to view ourselves.

> *"13 For You formed my inward parts;*
> *You covered me in my mother's womb.*
> *14 I will praise You, for I am fearfully and wonderfully made;*
> *Marvelous are Your works,*
> *And that my soul knows very well.*
> *15 My frame was not hidden from You,*
> *When I was made in secret,*
> *And skillfully wrought in the lowest parts of the earth.*
> *16 Your eyes saw my substance, being yet unformed.*
> *And in Your book they all were written,*
> *The days fashioned for me,*
> *When as yet there were none of them.*
> *17 How precious also are Your thoughts to me, O God!*
> *How great is the sum of them!*

Two — Growing Pains

¹⁸ If I should count them, they would be more in number than the sand;

When I awake, I am still with You." (Psalm 139:13-18 NKJV)

This is why the earliest teachings we receive are lessons on how to respect our bodies and those of others. Have you ever told or heard others instructing babies to "be gentle" when reaching for others? Schoolchildren are encouraged to "not hit," daughters and sons to "respect yourselves" and to "treat others the way you want to be treated"?

Why? Because by compromising that fundamental, we delve into a hole...or, better yet, a pit, like that of quicksand. On the surface, it doesn't seem so deep or detrimental. Not until we find ourselves sinking out of control and lowering to a state we never thought imaginable.

"Now faith is the substance of things hoped for, the evidence of things not seen."

HEBREWS 11:1 NKJV

Two — Growing Pains

Have you ever reached a point when you cry out with your hands in total surrender with one question, "WHY?!"

Why me? Why them? Why us? Why did you take…? Why did they do that? Why am I here? Why is this happening? – Trust me that in spite of the constant hurdles we find ourselves face to face with, we are never the only ones going through them. There is always someone going through something worse than what we would regard our own circumstances as. And in the midst of the storm we will rarely understand how the complexities of it will be played out, and why they happen, but one aspect of my life that remains unshaken is my faith and confidence in God.

While over the course of time, I can see how some situations allowed me to evolve as an individual, there are still some I've yet to understand the purpose behind and I may never end up figuring them out. I am certain though that these experiences created a vigor within me to help, where if I can prevent another from encountering the same results or aid in the recovery process to allow healing to take place faster than I did, I'll do so and it truly brings me joy and has brought me a stronger sense of empathy for people.

Pause & Consider = Selah

Everyone has challenges at one time or another. It's not if they are going to happen, it's when.

1. What obstacle(s) are you facing right now or have you faced in the past?

2. Can you recall a challenging time you faced and how you felt in the middle of it?

    a. How did you feel after a day passed? After a few weeks? After months or years?

    b. Do you realize how much progress you have made since?

    c. What are areas you still need breakthrough in?

3. Do you see yourself as a victor (overcoming the situation) or a victim (being trapped by it)?

Heavenly Father, I pray for the individual reading this chapter, that You would comfort them with Your perfect peace that surpasses all understanding. I ask that even now, wherever they are that You will cover them in the truth that Your word brings and that where death and negativity may have or may be running rampant in their lives' that You will reverse it and replace all the dark places with Your light and life. You have said in Your Word that, "The thief does not come except to steal, and to kill, and to destroy. I have come that they may have **life**, and that they may have *it* **more abundantly**." (John 10: 10 NKJV). I thank You that You will restore them to peace that will cover all aspects of their life, in Your mighty name we pray, Amen

Thoughts – Notes – Doodles

Three — Honest Admission

I can't remember leaving. I don't even remember getting home, or jumping into the shower. I must have slept, because I do remember how I felt when I woke up the next morning.

Numb.

A numbness reflecting the crippling reality of a world outside the rose-coloured hue I previously had on life.

"Did something happen yesterday?"

While a part of me knew the answer was yes, another part of me doubted that this page could even come out a chapter of my life story.

"Did something happen? What do I do next? Why does the

person staring at me in the mirror feel like a stranger? Sure I'm quiet, maybe not the most vocal of individuals, but I have integrity... I did have integrity. Is this still the guy I initially foresaw myself having a future with? How did things change so drastically in just a couple of weeks? Why am I so confused? He was such a gentleman when we met! He seemed perfect, so what happened?"

He invited me over to see where he lived. No harm in that. I saw him a few times before, on neutral territory, plus it was during the day and I had already planned for it to be a short visit, given that it was a bit of a journey. Little did I know—he had more in mind.

"Should I still be communicating with him? Should I end it? But how?! He's invited me over again, which means he didn't intentionally mean what took place before to happen, right? He likes me, and he really does value me, right? I'm not easy. I don't just put myself out like that! I even told myself after my last breakup that I am NOT, under any circumstances, going there with ANYBODY except my future husband. But now that that's gone out the window, I have to give this a fighting shot. He already knows me intimately."

Sadly, this charade went on for a month before I saw him for the last time. He met me at the door with the biggest grin on his face to make an announcement.

"You've won!"

Three — Honest Admission

"Won what?" I replied, confused at his excitement.

"You've won me! I wanted to find a good girl to have in my life. You beat the other girls I was seeing."

I could feel myself zoning out as I got pulled into my thoughts. Other girls? The numbness I felt from our initial rendezvous returned pulsing heavily through my entire body. I guess my reaction wasn't what he expected, because his eyebrows began to furrow. I can't even remember the details after that point. I recall mumbling some excuse to leave, shaking as I fumbled around for the keys to my car.

For what felt like the longest time afterwards, I felt empty. When I think back to that unforgettable day, I knew it wasn't a situation to even fathom returning to, but even though I wasn't a virgin with him, he took something that I couldn't get back. I didn't freely give it. It kind of reminds me of the time I had a bad hair day and this guy thought it would be funny to sneak up behind me, grab my hat and run away. I was mortified. I was uncovered, and an intimate part of myself that no one was supposed to see was exposed.

I didn't know anyone he may have paraded himself to as being the successor of his latest naïve conquest, but regardless, I felt naked and unprotected. Although he was the cause of this reproach, he provided a sense of covering—which was why I stayed. Now that it was over—I mean, come on—he was sleeping with multiple other women at the same time, the main character of a made-up reality show where the contestants didn't even realize they were being taken for a ride? ABSOLUTELY NOT! But that meant that I was alone. Alone, and emotionally naked. Alone, naked, and with a lot more time to be lost in my own thoughts, reflecting on just how worthless I felt.

I couldn't respect the person whose reflection peered at me in the mirror. How could I be so dumb, so naïve? The entire mess was on me. He was fine, and I was the vase he dropped, fragments of my shattered emotions flying in all directions. How could I be a victim if I went to his house? I was pursuing a relationship with this man. Obviously, I let things go too far, but even though I kept resisting, pushing him, and trying to pull away, I didn't scream for help. I wasn't held down at gunpoint, or drugged like in the movies. I was lying there in disbelief of what was actually happening.

Three — Honest Admission

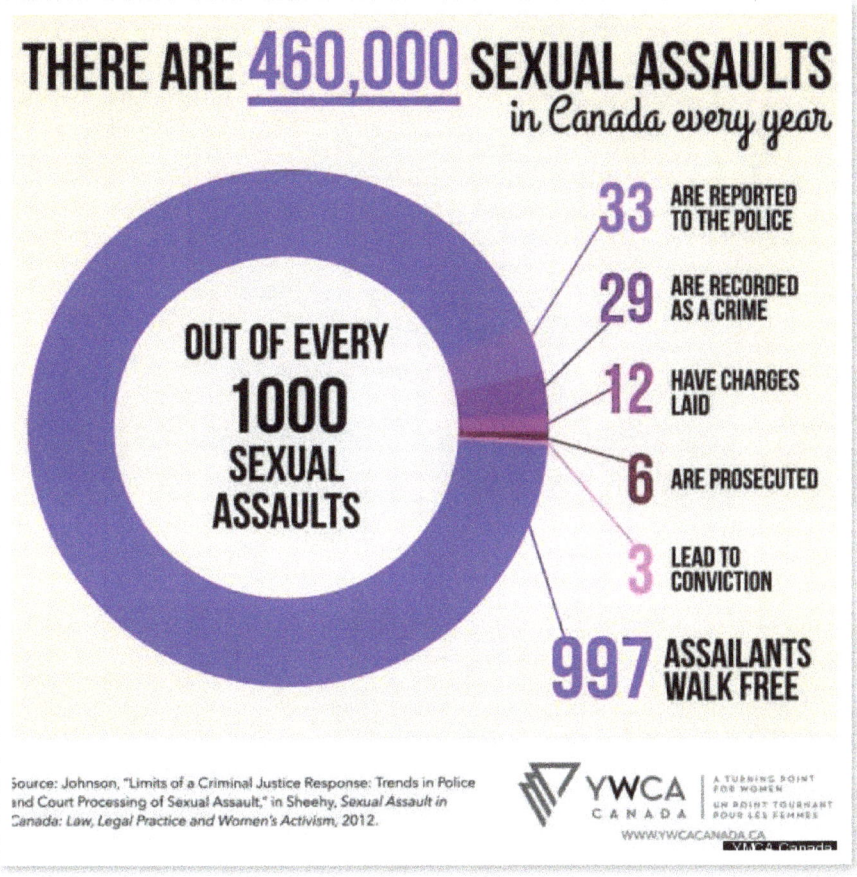

Now I'm one of those people. And when you look at the infographic displayed from women's service organization, YWCA Canada, highlighting the legal aspect of violence against women, and take particular notice of the fact that "only 33 out of every 1000 sexual assaults are reported to the police,", I'm inclined to believe that not only are these crimes not reported to police, most of them are not reported period…to anyone.

Why?

While I can't speak for every victim out there, I can speak for myself. Even though this happened to me, I was in denial for months that it really even occurred. If I barely believed myself, why would I risk the further humiliation I'd face if others didn't believe me either? I'd seen my share of highly-publicized court cases involving sexual assault, and unfortunately, even if the accusations are brought by credible witnesses, they are interrogated, cross-examined, and made out to be guiltier than the one who inflicted the assault. When you compare physical assault, even if the victim (against their better judgment) stays in a relationship with the abuser, the actions of the abuser are still considered to be wrong. It doesn't matter what the situation was that "warranted" the act. Placing your hands on someone to inflict harm, especially when the injured party isn't capable of defending themselves, is wrong. If this can be plainly understood, then why isn't same understood for the emotional and mental damage sustained when the abuse is sexual? If the contact was not consensual, then it was wrong. Whether the individual decides to stay or remain in contact with the individual or not has no bearing on whether the crime should be nullified. Rape is wrong. Sexual assault of any kind, by any person, at any time is wrong.

When I came to acknowledge and reluctantly accept what

Three — Honest Admission

happened to me, I had removed all contact information for my perpetrator to do anything about it. The intense desire not to revisit the memory in any way caused certain aspects of my life to stagnate, as the plot of this story thickens.

At first glance, the villain seems obvious to spot—but here's the twist. Much more difficult to identify was the incognito nemesis, sabotaging my recovery. The rape was the root of this problem, but the bigger enemy I had to confront was me. I couldn't face myself. I had self-esteem issues in the past, but this was on a whole other level! I didn't like who, or what, I saw. If I didn't even like myself at that point, how in God's Name could I face the One who put me on this earth?

> *"⁸ I cried out to you, Lord.*
> *I begged my Lord for mercy:*
> *⁹ "What is to be gained by my spilled blood,*
> *by my going down into the pit?*
> *Does dust thank you?*
> *Does it proclaim your faithfulness?*
> *¹⁰ Lord, listen and have mercy on me!*
> *Lord, be my helper!"*
> *¹¹ You changed my mourning into dancing.*

You took off my funeral clothes
and dressed me up in joy
¹² so that my whole being
might sing praises to you and never stop.
Lord, my God, I will give thanks to you forever."
(Psalm 30:8-12 CEB)

I've had battles with depression and suicidal thoughts in the past, but was never vocal about it because my mother suffered from it. Seeing how it affected her life, as well as ours, led me to never unload my burdens on her. However, speaking to her generically about some of my struggles was the best thing I could have done. With her similar firsthand experiences, she understood them best. Unbeknownst to her back then, our chats are what got me through many of those dark moments and are testament to how I was able to come out of them a victor. Since then, although I still have seasons where negative thoughts invade my mind, I know they are only moments, and the more that I focus on the beyond, rather than on the temporal, I'll recover much quicker. I must also highlight that there is true power in confession. The moment I expose the negative emotions I feel to my close circle of friends, the faster the cycle ends.

During that initial low phase, I managed to come to a place

Three — Honest Admission

where I could finally determine that my breath itself was valuable. But, I still was not sure about the rest of my life. My declaration to God was, "I'm done being the good girl whose dream was to find Mr. Right and get married and have kids. I'm "good," yet, get spit on. So, I am no longer taking any garbage from anyone. I'm going to just 'do me'.

I believed that I had that 'right'. Looking back on all that transpired, and reflecting on that first day at the condo, I realize that things got complicated really fast. You would think that after what happened, even if I never told anyone, I would have cut him off right there and then. But, I kept going back. I persisted in doing things I didn't really want to do, because—for a reason that makes no sense—I felt like I had to.

A sentiment echoed from my earlier relationship.

I became painfully aware that the fear of being trapped in that low mentality far outweighed not knowing what would happen if I left the relationship. Becoming a victim of this hurtful and humiliating treatment was a choice that I chose to make.

Ultimately, I didn't end up with him. He joined the growing list of men who were not right for me, and despite thinking my life was crumbling down around me, it didn't. Life went on. And whether or not *you* willingly choose or were forced to journey down a particular path in your life, life itself will continue nonetheless, regardless of you or me choosing to remain in negativity, or take a chance on something better. Looking back on that latest fiasco of a relationship with a sexually abusive partner, I was more than ready to take a stand. I came into a sense of self and purpose, though REALLY unrefined. Later on, I would learn that I was still hurt and in need of major healing. Hurting people hurt people—and I was no different.

"Pain leads to power. Struggle leads to strength. God uses every situation to make you better."

— UNKNOWN

Three — Honest Admission

I'm sure we have all faced an internal battle at one point or another. Not all of us get help from others when it's truly needed, instead choosing to face it alone. Everyone needs to have accountability—whether to a relative, close friend, spiritual advisor, mentor, or someone else. It is vitally important to make sure you have someone other than yourself to turn to when you need it. In a society that is so virtually connected, people lose the essence of what being truly connected feels like. I have a cousin who will say she needs to see "the whites of my eyes" to determine whether I am truly okay. The eyes never lie. Not only is it good to offload information, but it frees us from the weight of carrying burdens and keeping secrets or lies, restoring the power we need to overcome adversity back to us.

Pause & Consider = Selah

1. Who is your go-to person in times of trouble? Or who could you choose as an accountability partner?

2. Can you look back at significant periods when an accountability partner was beneficial, or would have been if you had one?

3. If you're struggling right now, and do not have someone to speak with, I implore you not to fight this battle alone. There are a growing number of resources available in many communities. You can reach out to a health care provider, as well as local crisis phone lines.

4. Know when to get immediate help!* If you:
    - Think about ending your life, or trying to end your life
    - Experience sensations that aren't real and/or beliefs that can't possibly be true

---

* Taken from http://www.heretohelp.bc.ca/factsheet/coping-with-mental-health-crises-and-emergencies#could%20i

- Make choices that put you in serious danger
- Become unable to care for yourself, and it's putting you at risk of serious harm
- Experience medication problems like serious side effects
- Experience an alcohol or any other drug overdose
- Take a dangerous combination of substances (like antianxiety medication and alcohol)

If you or a loved one experiences these signs, see your doctor right way, or call 911 or go to the nearest emergency room. If you call 911, don't leave anyone alone before emergency responders arrive. Wait until emergency responders say you can leave.

Lord, I thank You for providing scriptures such as 2 Corinthians 3:17 (NKJV) that states

> *[17] where the spirit of the Lord is there is liberty.*

This means that we are free from bearing the weight of our burdens as You said in Your word,

> *[28] Come to Me, all you who labor and are heavy laden, and I*

Three — Honest Admission

will give you rest. ²⁹ Take My yoke upon you and learn from Me, for I am gentle and lowly in heart, and you will find rest for your souls. ³⁰ For My yoke is easy and My burden is light." (Matthew 11:28-30 NKJV)

You never intended us to carry negative emotions such as depression, turmoil or heartache that would keep us hard pressed. I ask that You would reveal Your desire for us to find rest in our lives and leave the difficulties for You to assist us with as You intended. If there is a need for the individual reading this to find external help, I pray that You would direct them to the right place that they may find healing.

Thank You so much for loving us in spite of all the baggage we come with,

In Your Name we pray, Amen.

Thoughts – Notes – Doodles

Four — Brokenness

I wish I could say that the moment I mentally took stock of my life, light shone around me, demonstrating my conquering splendor, and that I was transformed into the heroic, cape-wearing warrior I mentioned at the onset of this story.

But, that's not the case. I took a stand, but not one that leaned on God. My objective was terrible. I determined to leave a path of broken men behind me, treating them the way they treated me in the past. I moved into the next phase of my brokenness, which I'd like to entitle, *Bitterness*—though it was no musical. I was mad. But, this is the revelation I received. Yes, I was mad that men could be so hurtful—but even more so, I was mad at myself for allowing others to get close enough to hurt me. My attitude became shallow. I decided I'd talk to whoever I pleased, and move on to the next when it suited me. Thank God, that phase was short lived. Although I felt justified in my logic, it still didn't feel quite right within. What I actually did was create a new façade to escape the reality of the hurt I felt.

It's amazing how inner pain can be so intent on causing others damage. When we run away from dealing with the source of our pain and frustration, it becomes like that age old adage I mentioned before: "hurting people hurt people." Only when we hone in on that pain will we feel reprieve from it. Like the physiotherapy I underwent following a car accident I had, I learned that facing the pain head-on is the only way progress can be made. It's natural to run from things that make us feel uncomfortable, and nurse our wounds by protecting them from any form of sensory engagement, but by doing so we weaken the affected parts of our body, ultimately increasing the time it takes to heal.

Anyone who has experienced God working in their lives can attest to His sense of humor. No sooner than I made my declaration, my first "victim" approached me at the gas station. While paying for my gas, a guy behind me said, "she's paying for mine too." I didn't even glance back as I walked to my car, but he was persistent. He knocked on the passenger side window for me to roll

Four — Brokenness

it down. Without delving into any of my personal info, he asked for my number. 'Who does this guy think he is,' I thought to myself.

"Just like that, you're asking for my phone number?" I responded.

"Well, I could keep you here, and talk about how pretty you are, how nice your eyes are, and how I'd like to know you better—but you look like you're busy with places to go and ultimately I'd ask you for your number anyway. So, why not get straight to the point?"

I tell everyone that I've heard tons of corny lines, both in my own life and from my friends' experiences. "Hey baby in blue" is one I'll always remember, walking through Scarborough Town Center in my baby blue FUBU football jersey. Another one was "How you so sexy, you must drink Pepsi!" Never had someone approach me so bluntly before, and though it lacked finesse, I appreciated the sincerity. Even so, I still had my radar up, ready to shatter whatever dreams this man thought he had with me. At this point, I wasn't interested in anything serious. So, you can imagine my response when each and every time I spoke with this man after that, he greeted me as his "future wife." It honestly infuriated me. Why call me that? That was the label I wanted men in my past to place on me, and they didn't. Now, when I finally concluded that I'd never have that life—never be wife material—and I was comfortable with my newly minted role as *Miss Independent,* who definitely didn't need a man... this guy came to mock me? I fought with him, and myself. I even almost succeeded in my plan to take vengeance on prior men by making this man the first victim of my intentional abuse. But, at the last moment, when I thought he would walk after countless psychological blows, it's as if God put a mirror in front of me to see exactly what I was doing.

It wasn't nice.

I was becoming someone I truly wasn't, inflicting pain on others—something I previously would have never encouraged. God knew I was damaged, but not beyond repair. Before I could put myself in a worse position, he intervened by bringing this man into my life, to shake me up a little. A man who, not perfect by any means, had his own refining process to undergo, but genuinely pursued me. Almost nine years from that initial encounter, I will always see how God used him to save me from myself in that vulnerable stage.

> *[9] and finally He said to me, "My grace is enough to cover and sustain you. My power is made perfect in weakness." So ask me about my thorn, inquire about my weaknesses, and I will gladly go on and on—I would rather stake my claim in these*

and have the power of the Anointed One at home within me. *[10] I am at peace and even take pleasure in any weaknesses, insults, hardships, persecutions, and afflictions for the sake of the Anointed because when I am at my weakest, He makes me strong. (2 Corinthians 12:9-10 VOICE)*

Our courtship was not without its difficulties. I was still learning how to love myself again, and when it came to others, people-pleasing was still in effect. I always ran around helping others—whether it meant picking up my high school ex, who had since apologized for his abusive behaviour and agreed to part on civil terms, or dealing with my mother who needed support, or my father, who began to grow distant. Anyone who called on me for anything, really. It took re-evaluation to realize that there would be moments when I needed to take time out to pursue the things I wanted. I could not be available to everyone all of the time. This became a paradigm shift in most of my relationships. Because of that my father (who my sister and I lived with at that time) for the first time ever, enforced a curfew.

I was twenty-four years old.

To give some background into this new dilemma, let me explain…

During the time I experienced turmoil at the home of my father and stepmother in Brampton, my stepmother started increasingly taking up sides with my ex. Together, they would berate me, speaking about me as if I wasn't there, and constantly question why I was still around. Many days, I spent hours "sleeping" to lessen the pain of being awake. I've mentioned before that in our home was the tradition of isolating people. If one was deemed "bad," no one else should communicate with them, or else they too would become excommunicated. If, for whatever reason, someone else became the centre of negative attention, you became so relieved to no longer be the main outcast at that moment that you would support everyone else, even if you disagreed.

After much reflection, I see now that both my stepmother and father were broken in ways I couldn't see. Even though I would frequently ask my father if I should just leave and go live with my mother, he would respond that I was being spiritually tested and I needed to stay and fight it out!

Despite the turmoil we lived in, I cared deeply for every one of them. You could look at it as the kind of feelings members have for their gang affiliations. You want so much to feel like you belong somewhere, that you'll accept the subpar treatment that's given you at times. I felt an overwhelming sense of responsibility for my

Four — Brokenness

stepmother's unhappiness. She had said the only reason why she got married and was still around was because I cried. It caught her off guard years before, when she mentioned to me that she planned to leave. She and my father decided to get married, and it seemed she had regretted it ever since. I clearly remember the night we were at Erev Shabbat services. She told us she would meet us there. Something felt off…It was unsettling and I couldn't put my finger on it. We weren't even on good speaking terms, and yet I called her in the middle of service. She answered, saying that she was running late. When we got home, the situation became clear. Items were missing. Her clothes were gone. Linens had vanished from the closet. It was surreal, almost as if our home was broken into, with no chance of vindication. My father's response was one of strength—the same resilient demeanour he used to present the congregation with a commentary—that is, until it came time to formally address the congregation about what happened. For the first time, my father's cover was blown. His brokenness was apparent for all to see. I sat watching in confusion. Up until then, I never regarded my father as a man. No, he was superhuman. He was always fine.

Shortly after that, I told him about my ex's behaviour. He reacted almost immediately, telling him to leave. From then, the house was put up for sale and we had to pack everything up, storing them at a friend's as we tried to figure out where we would go. My sister still had one year of high school left in Brampton, and I was working in Mississauga. My father went to go stay with a friend in Toronto. After briefly staying with friends near our old house, my sister went to live with her best friend, and I went to live with my mother. The relationship as mother-daughter was healing and for the first time, I saw the good traits I acquired from my mother, and celebrated those qualities. It wasn't a long term living arrangement, though. Once my father got back on his feet, he secured a 2 bedroom basement apartment and I moved back there. Once she graduated, my sister joined us.

The damage was done, though. Our relationships were different. A mentality took precedence in our family, where the focus would be fixed so hard on one thing, that everything else around was dismissed. We were fragmented, with little cross-communication between each of us during the period that we were all in our various locations. My sister and I had grown apart in the Brampton house, but once we left that home behind, we slowly rebuilt our relationship as grown women. We both loved to walk, so that's how it began. We would often walk all around my mother's apartment building, from floor to floor, just talking. Eventually, we circled the same area so many times that we decided to change things up and walk around

Four — Brokenness

the neighbourhood. For some strange reason, this always happened to be at night, but it gave us the opportunity to learn more about the Cederbrae area. We ended up making Coffee Time our destination spot. Through our constant talks, getting to learn more about each other again and keeping up that communication even when we were living apart, we grew into great friends. My father was different. I no longer felt the same bond that we had before. I had made it a point to keep connected, and we spoke regularly—but once we were all living together again, the changes became clear. He would do everything by himself. No longer did he prioritize doing things as a family. We still attended services, but the laughter and smiling stopped once we were back home.

When I met my friend at the gas station, I introduced him to my mother. In fact, within weeks, she had to move—he and his friend came to help us do it. Due to my father's standards, however, I felt the introduction to him would need more careful thought and preparation. I decided that bringing him to service would be the best way for this meeting to happen. What I learned from this experiment is that, no matter the place you choose, when it comes to a father and his DAUGHTER, no place will ever be perfect. ☺

My father was civil with Richie during the service, but shortly thereafter, the curfew was initiated. It made no sense to me at all. There was barely a call initiated by him, from week to week to check on us while we were separated—and now that we were back together, and I was doing what I thought was reasonable by keeping him informed about my relationship, I was being punished for it? Although my sister also had a boyfriend, he had been in the picture throughout her high school days, so this sudden change was definitely brought on by me. Nonetheless, Richie respected the time and made sure I always left him to get back on time. Not wanting my sister to get into any trouble, I would leave extra early to get her from wherever she was, too. We were so different in that way. She was fearless, unafraid of repercussions or consequences—I, on the other hand, was the complete opposite! I hated getting into trouble. You can probably imagine the response when I came home and told my dad that I was engaged!

One night, we made it home on time, but couldn't get into the house. The locks were changed! After trying, without success, to climb onto the roof of my car to open a kitchen window, we resorted to ringing the doorbell. I went from feeling like a ninja who could pull off cool feats, to doing the walk of shame. My father didn't say a word as he opened the door, and went back to the basement. By this time, he owned the entire house and we were staying upstairs—but when we got to our bedrooms, they were empty! After looking

Four — Brokenness

around, we found all our stuff from both of our rooms piled up in our previous single bedroom in the basement. We had to wade through the chaos to create a bed to crash for the night. I'm sure it was at that point that my sister refused to stay in those living conditions and sought to move out. As challenging as everything was, now that Richie and I were engaged, I wanted to get married first before moving in. But, in light of a discovery, my sister helped me begin to think more intently about the conditions I was in because…

I was now carrying my first child.

"You are strong enough to face it all, even if it doesn't feel like it right now." — UNKNOWN

Four — Brokenness

Have you ever looked back at certain times of your life, wondering how you ever made it through, thankful that it's over, and praying that you never encounter such an ordeal again?

It's such a relief to be out on the other side, isn't it!

Do you realize that—although you're happy it's over—beyond coming out sporting new cuts and scrapes, you actually grew?

I liken this to when I speak to my children about school. They may start out a new school year feeling overwhelmed. Everything is challenging and new, but once summer arrives, if they speak of feeling any anxiety, it's in reference to the year to come—not when recounting the year they just finished.

Strength is gained through every hardship, even when we don't feel that way. My personal message to my children, and to you, or anyone else experiencing something similar, is that you need only to **remain confident, knowing that despite the outcome, every challenge that comes your way is a means of** drawing out the strength that lies dormant within you.

Pause & Consider = Selah

1. There tends to be a direct correlation between brokenness and breakthrough.

    a. What do you feel you lost through difficulty?

    b. What do you feel that you have gained through it?

2. What aspects of yourself have been strengthened due to difficult circumstances you have faced?

3. Remind yourself of the power that increases within you every time you are faced with new obstacles.

Heavenly Father, I am grateful that Your plans for us far outweigh those we see for ourselves. I ask that You will equip the individual reading this right now with the endurance and determination to prevail against every challenge that comes their way. And I ask that you will cause them to move from break ups and breakdowns to breakthroughs in their lives,

In Your mighty Name we pray, Amen.

Thoughts – Notes – Doodles

Five — Transition

Shortly after acquiring the position of youth leader in my congregation, I participated in my first cross-border youth retreat. We arrived and settled into shared accommodations. I began to notice that I wasn't feeling quite like my usual self, but I blamed it on the journey from Ontario, Canada to Pennsylvania, U.S.A., where the retreat was to take place. I was exhausted and felt ill. No matter what I did over the next few days, I could not shake the nausea. It prevented me from taking part in many of the activities I had wanted to. Nonetheless, I still took up my turn of driving us all back home once the weekend was over, stopping frequently to keep my caffeine levels topped up.

During a conversation at work the following Monday, my coworkers suspected that I was pregnant. Unable to fathom the possibility, I refused to take their advice and check if it were true. The following week, I still couldn't shake the constant "off" feeling, and though I still dismissed the belief that I was pregnant, I went to get checked out at a local walk-in clinic. The doctor requested bloodwork be done, and I'll never forget the day I received the call from their office to come in as soon as I could. Every possible scenario played in my head. I feared the worst—was I dying? Had I come down with some terrible ailment that I'd have to live with for the rest of my life?

The doctor sat me down in the examination room with a solemn expression on his face. He revealed my results, which showed that I was indeed pregnant— and unexpectedly so. He proceeded to ask whether I wanted to terminate. Pause. It's amazing how the mind works. My life was in upheaval. I had recently been accepted into a post-secondary program for audio engineering, and was trying to figure out what arrangements were necessary to attend this school, located in London, Ontario. I had just gotten engaged a month prior, and we were in the middle of visiting venues to figure things out for a proposed wedding date of May the following year. I thought I was going to receive news of a terminal illness. Although we had discussed children, it was not on my immediate to-do list—yet, there wasn't a single doubt in my mind as to whether I'd go through with

Five — Transition

having this child. Despite the *fabulous* timing, there was no error in this. Despite my lack of experience with babies and children, I accepted my gift of impending motherhood and went straight to my fiancé to deliver the shocking news.

You could say that my physical experience involved pretty standard pregnancy ailments, from aversion to meat, nausea every time the car jolted, to tenderness and bloating—not to mention extreme fatigue—which did not help with my job at the gym, where I had to arrive before 5am to open five days out of the week.

However, the emotional and mental battle that ensued, mostly unspoken, was intense. One of first things we had to tackle was revealing the news to my Rabbi, who we were scheduled to see the next week for pre-marital counselling. To say he was displeased would be an understatement. He mostly voiced his disappointed in me, and was livid towards my fiancé. I was forced to step down from all the ministries I was involved in immediately. I could not even share with the youth why I was leaving them. Up to this day, that is my biggest regret. I hate that I left without giving them the explanation they deserved to have, so they'd know that I didn't just abandon them. I didn't want them to believe I thought little of my commitment to be there for them. I also wanted to be transparent—to allow them to see me as a regular human being who makes decisions that won't always be the popular choice. But, wanting to be obedient to leadership, I kept silent.

I hated being in any kind of spotlight, especially the negative kind. But this situation put me on display again and again. Even now, I am sometimes mistaken for a schoolgirl—so you can imagine the comments I received when I was eight years younger! I didn't plan on telling anyone, not even my sister—until she heard me say that I was craving water, and she asked if I was pregnant or something. The expression on my face gave me away! She became my main source of support. My mother was not pleased, initially, upset at what had been *done* to her daughter. My friends didn't understand why I didn't feel like going out anymore and why I was always too "sick." My fiancé—who stopped attending my congregation after their negative behaviour towards him—was less than understanding of the emotional turmoil I was going through, and the added stress created even more discord between us.

When I look back at the treatment I received from people in my congregation after stepping down, I think some of them would have greatly appreciated if I crawled in a corner somewhere and never came back. The board decided that although I was engaged prior to the pregnancy, I could no longer get married there (a place I had attended for just shy of ten years, by the way). An example was made

Five — Transition

out of me. They thought marrying us would encourage others to do the same if found in similar circumstances. When I attended prayer meetings, I was the subject of congregational prayers against the ungodly by individuals in leadership. They prayed against "heathens" who corrupted their holy place. They avoided me, as though any interaction would subject them to catching a plague. Nonetheless, I made a point not to miss services. I didn't do this to be a thorn in their sides each week, but rather because shedding my titles of ministry allowed me to stop acting and being for others, and start being just for God. I can't remember a time, since I professed my faith at thirteen years old, when I was *not* involved in some type of ministry. Now I was able to close my eyes and tune everything and everyone around me out, focusing on why I was there. In those trying and hurtful moments I felt God whispering to my heart.

I was twenty-four years old and in deep conflict. An argument flared up, ending with my father stating that he was being used for his home. This was said, despite the fact that we had paid our way. Since I was planning on getting married, my sister left. Once she packed to leave, I determined that I couldn't continue living there anymore, even though co-living before I was married was not something I really wanted to do. Now excommunicated from my father, I avoided placing additional worry on my mother, who was sick again and admitted to the hospital. I had no relatives nearby, apart from my sister. I tried to figure out how, when and if I was even getting married, and overwhelmed by the reality that in less than a year, I'd be a mother!

There were many moments where doubt got a foothold of me. I began to think that God had gotten this one wrong. I don't know why He thought that I, Chantai Finesse, a young, confused, and unequipped woman could undertake all of this! Yet, every time, and even now, when I feel like the water is rising above my throat and I start to panic, gasping for air, a scripture I discovered in my teens floods back to my mind,

> "[26] ...but now He has promised, saying, "Yet once more I shake not only the earth, but also heaven." [27] Now this, "Yet once more," indicates the removal of those things that are being shaken, as of things that are made, that the things which cannot be shaken may remain..." (Hebrews 12:26-27 NKJV)

Since then, every time my life shakes up, I liken it to this scripture. I remember that God's plans for me often require a drastic shift; one that wouldn't occur by playing it safe. Despite my personal belief

Five — Transition

in myself, there must be more to me than I can see. Through the drama, I persevered. It reached a point where I thought my fiancé and I were at our end. I left it up to him to determine whether we'd get married at all, and to my surprise, he contacted a minister who arranged to marry us onsite at a place of our choosing. After considering our options, we decided to keep it small and simple—doing it right in our apartment!

I remember it well. My sister (whose birthday fell on the day before our wedding) spent time creating floral bouquets and hanging decorations and for the two of us. I still have the bouquets to this very day. One of my sister-in-laws was all hands on deck, helping with everything from moving our living room furniture into the second bedroom with my fiancé's cousins help, to setting up chairs and putting up décor. It was the middle of July. Though I think we had a window AC unit, the place was HOT! My sister and one of my friends ensured that my hair and makeup was on point. When my mother went missing, my sister had to go find her! It was something, I'll tell you that! I didn't even walk up to any music, as we started later than anticipated. I was too nervous by that point to really care. My wedding band didn't even fit, as my friend's mother gave us both wedding bands until we could afford the ones we desired. My father never showed up. He said he didn't know about it, despite us calling, texting, leaving messages, and even hand delivering an invitation to his door. It was an intimate gathering, but I'm so appreciative for those who came to support us that day. We didn't have much, but our loved ones rallied around us. If you were to look at the photography a friend captured for us as a wedding gift, you'd never know about all the drama that ensued behind the scenes.

One of things I loved about being married was being able to flash my ring anytime I heard a comment or saw people looking at my growing belly. Currently, there are times I will take off and or even forget to wear my ring when running out, but the security that I have now is a far cry from what I possessed back then. There was still much progress to be made, especially regarding the shame I carried around. Although we were married, it was only one step in the journey to rid myself of the shame that had taken a hold of me from my past. Getting married would never be able to undo all the difficulties and heartache I endured before.

I spent a great deal of time battling old inhibitions. My husband constantly reminded me that we were equal partners. It was crazy! As a single individual, I expressed strength of mind, focus, and independence, but the second I was in a relationship, I shifted back into the state of mind I had as a youth. I looked to him for everything. Whenever I was going to make a purchase, I would call

Five — Transition

him if he wasn't around and ask for his permission—to which he'd always respond, do what you need to do! I can recall once asking him for directions to get to somewhere I already knew. It was as if the person I truly was began to drown again, not knowing how to infuse the independence and focus of my singularity into a relationship, balancing it with co-dependency.

My husband and I have twelve years between us, and so my appearance became another point of contention. I wrestled with this when we were out together, or with his friends. To overcome, I began to dress differently than I normally would, opting for a less youthful wardrobe. In hindsight, I create a new concept of how Chantai Finesse, *wife and soon-to-be Mother* should appear and behave. Unfortunately, I lacked in confidence and appreciation for myself, never realizing that all I had to be was me. Aside from the internal adjustments, I also became deafeningly aware of the changes that occur after marriage. I lost friends! Many of the people who were so close to me before began to drift during the engagement period, and then they vanished once I added the 'r' between Ms. to become a *Mrs*. It felt lonely. To that mix, add the emotional whirlwind from being pregnant and the results were many tearful episodes, rolling in like the tide on a beach.

There were a few changes in my congregation. After the wedding, some people at the synagogue became a little more engaging. I was subjected to less social chastisement. In fact, some of the members threw me a surprise baby shower. Imagine my astonishment when those who had ridiculed me before, then remarked, "Of course we were going to throw you a shower!" It was deemed fitting to mention that—although I had now "rectified" my situation— this pregnancy occurred out of wedlock, and I was described as the one who "got caught" to all the people who were newer to the congregation. All who happened to be there on the day of the shower got full disclosure of my situation. I was grateful then that my stepmother made a habit of putting me in uncomfortable situations growing up. I'm not sure whether it was to teach me to adjust to anything, or if it merely brought her enjoyment to see me flustered as I tried to recover from the embarrassment. Either way, it taught me to realize that others would feel the need to highlight my shortcomings, probably due to consciousness of their own flaws. I accepted that I was being made an example of, without taking on the humiliation they may secretly have hoped for. Regardless of what people thought of me at that point, God drew close to me in a way that I had never experienced Him before, and it was all part of the process to fulfill an unrealized goal.

Five — Transition

⁹And He has said to me, "My grace is sufficient for you, for power is perfected in weakness." Most gladly, therefore, I will rather boast about my weaknesses, so that the power of Christ may dwell in me. ¹⁰ Therefore I am well content with weaknesses, with insults, with distresses, with persecutions, with difficulties, for Christ's sake; for when I am weak, then I am strong. (2 Corinthians 12:9-10 NASB)

"The strongest action for a woman is to love herself and shine amongst those who never believed she could."

— AUTHOR UNKNOWN

Five — Transition

I never realized until much later just how much strength I possessed from carrying that tiny being of life within me. There was so much hope and anticipation for my unborn child that kept me constantly ready for battle.

Before becoming pregnant, I was more susceptible to bearing the expectations of others but here I was beginning to draw lines in my mental sand of what I would accept as my child's mother and choosing to do things that I believed would benefit him or her.

Our lives have the ability to obtain unfathomable reach but if we chose to reside in the prison of what others project on us we do ourselves a disservice. The eyeful I received from those who sought my downfall were met with a response of resilience. Despite how frail I felt within, it was my external reactions that people observed and it spoke volumes.

Pause & Consider = Selah

1. How do you respond when faced with conflict?

    a. Do you listen to your inner self/voice?

    b. Do you identify others' perceptions of you?

2. Are you truly living your life for yourself?

    a. Do you struggle with how you identify yourself?

3. What are one (or more) truths about yourself that you are unapologetic for? (e.g. *I'm opinionated, I'm loyal, I'm trustworthy, I like to make jokes…*)

    a. Focus on these and list three positive attributes about each truth (e.g. For I'm trustworthy = I make people feel safe, I'm responsible, I have close relationships)

Dear Lord, I thank you for building character in each of us. Where we have faced trials in our lives is reminiscent of precious stones tested by fire. I pray that as You continue to refine us through the various challenges we face, You will remove all insecurities and negative mindsets, actions and self-sabotaging ways so that our true inner diamond will be reflected underneath. Thank you for Isaiah 43:18-19a (NLT) which tells us (regarding our previous ways),

> [18] "But forget all that—it is nothing compared to what I am going to do. [19] For I am about to do something new. See, I have already begun! Do you not see it?"

We eagerly wait for the good you work within us to be revealed, and we ask You to help us to be patient until it does,

In Your Name we pray, Amen.

Thoughts – Notes – Doodles

Six — Zariyah

On the morning of the congregational baby shower, there were signs that labour was imminent. But, I was a novice. The ladies I told said it was nothing, especially since I was three weeks away from my due date. Imagine my surprise when I woke up that same night, after feeling a 'pop.' I got up and found slight, yet constant, dripping. Wondering if that is what it meant to have your water break, I went to the living room and called the hospital. I didn't want to alarm my husband or sister who were both asleep. The nurse I spoke with chalked it up to nothing. Since I wasn't feeling any significant pain, she felt there was no reason to come in, and that if my water did break, I would *definitely* know it. I hung up and got up from the couch. What followed felt like something out of a typical movie. I ran to the bathroom screaming for my husband, who slipped in a puddle when he entered the hallway confused, half-asleep and bewildered at the chaos so early in the morning! My sister, the logical type, asked if I was in any pain. I answered no, and she said, "Okay, there's time," and went back to bed. I, on the other hand, excitedly got ready with my bag of belongings, checklist and hubby in tow as we rushed to the hospital. I was going to be a mother!

Once checked into triage, we waited with me laying uncomfortably on a stretcher for someone to attend to us. An alarm sounded, and "CODE PINK" came over the pager, followed by a loud cry in the hallway near us and a woman screaming, "don't take my baby!" I was already the type of individual who doesn't enjoy going to the hospital. These weren't panning out to be the kind of memories I pictured myself recalling about the day I brought my firstborn into the world. But, they also highlighted the reality of what was happening. We were about to bring a child into an imperfect world. No longer was I focused on whether it would be boy or girl (the child had shielded this knowledge throughout the entire pregnancy). All we wanted now was to have a safe delivery and a healthy baby.

Hours later, after repeated checks, an IV hook-up, and monitoring, they determined that our baby was not quite ready to make an appearance. So, I was discharged. They suggested that I walk around

Six — Zariyah

and see if labour could be jumpstarted that way. I left, wearing a diaper, and with the IV still in my hand. The first thought that came to mind was how hungry I was. I did the obvious and organized a "last breakfast" at Markham Station with my friends to celebrate my last meal sans child and satisfy my cravings for French toast and egg sandwiches, a meal I frequently enjoyed throughout the pregnancy, catered by one of my besties. For some reason, my list of cravings included breakfast, dessert and candies. Once back home, I went to sleep. The excitement tired me out, and with labour being so close, I figured I should get some rest—forget about walking around the mall. We later returned to the hospital and they suggested to induce. I figured, why not get the ball rolling?

I was nowhere near prepared for the discomfort that comes with inducing labour. I thrive on being in control. When I'm not, I am completely out of element—especially when it concerned myself. I hated having my body manipulated by dials on a machine. I began sweating as the machine determined when I would feel my next wave of pain. It was not pleasant, and not what I foresaw for myself at all.

Long before my pregnancy, I pictured going through labour without an epidural or any pain relief. My mindset was that women have given birth for millenniums, and that—for the most part—our bodies were created to withstand the process from conception to delivery. Even when I considered that some women experienced complications, requiring medical intervention, this is not the case for all. I don't believe the mentality of an expectant mother should be to expect the worse, unless there is a valid cause for concern. I did okay using my own coping mechanisms, until I met the OB-GYN who would be present for my labour. She came in to check on me and when she realized that I had already declined the epidural, she told me that I had hours left to go that would be far worse than what I was already feeling. She said that by the time I was ready to push, I would be too fatigued to do so leaving my unborn child at a higher risk of dying!

Yeah, try swallowing all of that!

After enduring her ridicule of my choice, my confidence began to wane even more. Both my husband and mother concluded that I wouldn't be able to do it. With only my sister's reassurance, I buckled under the negative opinions and got the epidural. When it came time to push, I couldn't feel anything. Relying on the nurses instructions was difficult, because I had no sensation from the waist down. The doctor told me that my child would die if I didn't push, as they no longer waited to advise me when contractions came. Near the end, my baby's shoulder got stuck on her way out. Two nurses

Six — Zariyah

jumped up and down, applying pressure to my stomach to free her. Finally, she was out! I had my baby girl—and bore the bruises and stitches to prove it!

Everything was a daze after that! A surreal moment, gazing down at all 6lbs and 7oz., of this tiny being. Every emotion imaginable raced through my body. Almost 10 months of pregnancy is something in and of itself, but none of it even remotely prepared me for the actual transition that takes place once a child is born. I had my list of names, both male and female, with me and once our baby girl was nestled in my arms, the names we chose for her almost leapt off of the page.

Zariyah Adaya – Princess, Adorned / Treasured by God.

She was the picture of absolute beauty. Tiny, flawless, and full of life. Truly, a gift was bestowed on us. The effects of the epidural prevented me from maneuvering very much, but as we settled into the recovery ward, they discovered that my princess had jaundice, and so she was placed under the UV light to help her recover. We were stuck in the hospital for what felt like an eternity, waiting to hear that she was healthy enough to go home. My heart ached. She was kept in an incubator under UV lights most of the time, wearing only a diaper and an eye covering. I couldn't bear to hear her cry, so I kept picking her up, hoping she wouldn't feel alone and abandoned. I stayed mindful of her limited understanding of the drastic change from the warmth of my womb to the cold, loud and unfamiliar world she was now a part of. She didn't know what was going on around her. Although I could see her, my new motherly instincts surged at every sound uttered, no matter how faint, from her lips. Like most new parents, I kept getting up to watch her chest rise and fall. I wanted to make sure she was breathing. Holding her brought us both immediate comfort, but it only delayed the improvements they wanted to see. So, we spent the next few days in the hospital. And was I ready to leave! It felt so lonely being the only patients in the room. Visitors were limited due to the H1N1 pandemic, causing the hospital to be in a semi-restricted state. Finally, the good news came that we would be discharged, 4 days after she was born. My husband and sister came to collect us. Exhausted and relieved, I didn't expect the great number of gifts that we found waiting upon our arrival home. This being our first child together, and my husband's first daughter, he had gone on a shopping spree for dresses and all things pink and frilly for his new baby girl. He surprised me with gifts too!

Out of the hospital and back in our own environment, I began

Six — Zariyah

to realize how much my life had shifted. I shared responsibility for directly impacting this very new life. As we got Zariyah acquainted with her new home, I became reacquainted with my own significance in a very different way.

> *⁴ But God, who is rich in mercy, because of His great love with which He loved us, ⁵ even when we were dead in trespasses, made us alive together with Christ (by grace you have been saved), ⁶ and raised us up together, and made us sit together in the heavenly places in Christ Jesus, ⁷ that in the ages to come He might show the exceeding riches of His grace in His kindness toward us in Christ Jesus. ⁸ For by grace you have been saved through faith, and that not of yourselves; it is the gift of God, ⁹ not of works, lest anyone should boast. ¹⁰ For we are His workmanship, created in Christ Jesus for good works, which God prepared beforehand that we should walk in them. (Ephesians 2:4-10 NKJV)*

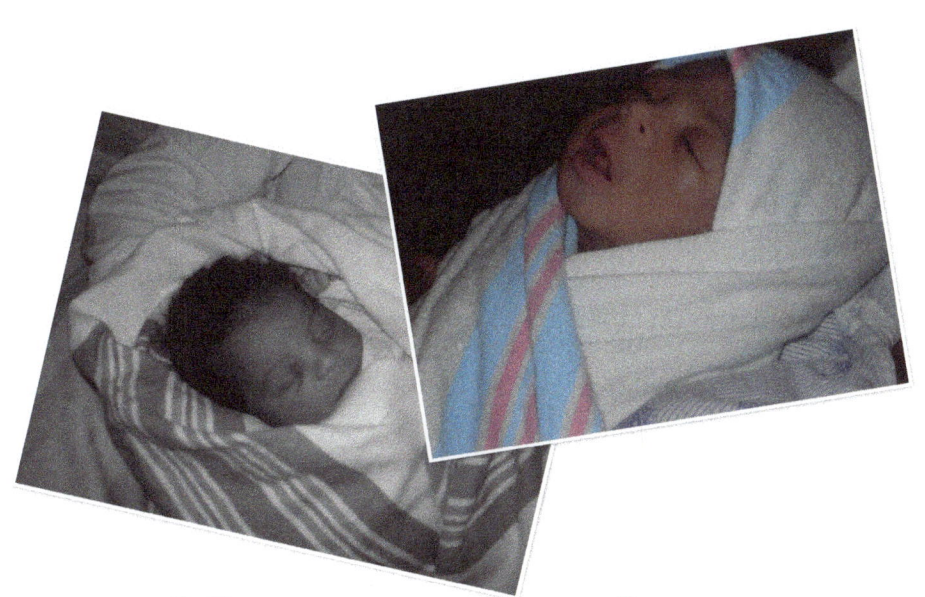

"Sometimes you have to be your own hero"

Six — Zariyah

Will we ever truly be ready for all the hurdles thrown at us? While the answer is a resounding no, we must acknowledge our imperfections—and know that having them is perfectly okay. We must learn to stand after falling. We must also learn what to avoid after experiencing pain, and how to jump with both feet in the air celebrating after succeeding at something new.

I had three children after my first. With each pregnancy my birthing experience improved from the one before it. Zariyah's birth served as my induction into the chaotic, overwhelming and incredible new world of parenting. I learned that I would fail at my own plans, but still find ways to make it work. The expectations I placed on others? They would not always be fulfilled, but I found that I could trust in myself more and that I didn't give myself nearly enough credit. I, along with everyone else, have a natural ability to adapt to situations—even *if* I didn't have the latest books with the best methods or the time to keep abreast of the latest trends. None of that meant that I was incapable of doing a great job.

The lesson learned? **Do not be afraid**.

Pause & Consider = Selah

1. What are you afraid of?

2. How do your fears hold you back?

3. How do you see yourself overcoming your fears?

4. "You are BRAVER than you believe, STRONGER than you seem, SMARTER than you think, and LOVED more than you'll ever know" – A.A. Milne

    Affirmations are great tools to use to change your way of thinking.

    a. Find a quote of your choice (you can use the one above if you'd like) and repeat it *out loud* every day for the next 30 days

    b. How did you feel after repeating the quote on day 1? Day 15? Day 30?

Dear Lord, thank you for empowering us through our discomforts. I pray that you will help the soul reading this right now to recognize their struggles in a new light, and not be defeated by it. Instead, help them to have a renewed vision so they can see how to subdue and rise above it.

In Your Name we pray, Amen.

Thoughts – Notes – Doodles

Seven — Treasured

How could such a tiny being possess such assurance and confidence in me, a blindsided new mother? It was mesmerizing. I read countless articles and books. I even watched many shows on pregnancy, childbirth, and babies, but let me tell you how unprepared I was for what came after labour!

Motherhood proved to be an internal battle for me. I placed high expectations on myself and I constantly fell short! Zariyah was an amazing baby, but I had only changed a diaper once before I had her. Breastfeeding was a nightmare in the beginning. I felt like a failure. Sometimes I felt an overwhelming weight pressing down on me, telling me what a terrible job I did as a mother. I'd ask my husband if he thought I was doing okay and though he'd say yes, it wasn't enough. He couldn't understand why I'd be in tears. Looking back to those days, I remember the mixed emotions I felt every time I picked up my Princess. Despite my doubts, I possessed the comfort and love she needed, and that was enough for her to settle in my arms.

During that period, the theme of my life focused on God's purpose for me—He viewed me as His own treasured princess! I was being built up to recognize God's view of me. In spite of my shortcomings I determined to overcome them to be the best mother I could be to Zariyah, He, in His infinite power and glory, showed me that I could be confident in resting in His sure and steady arms.

God used her then, and continues to use my now eight-year-old daughter to remind me of how He views me as a treasure: His princess whom He adores.

God caused me to stir, awakening a powerful truth that was evident from my own conception and birth, but had faded as my spirit wore down by the circumstances I faced. I wasn't a princess in His eyes because of anything I did—I was His princess regardless. Created and chosen to be the unique, flawed, overly-detailed, questioning, and often quirky individual that I am. Perfectly imperfect, crowned as a daughter of the Most High!

[28] And we know that all things work together for good to

Seven — Treasured

those who love God, to those who are the called according to His purpose. ²⁹ For whom He foreknew, He also predestined to be conformed to the image of His Son, that He might be the firstborn among many brethren. ³⁰ Moreover whom He predestined, these He also called; whom He called, these He also justified; and whom He justified, these He also glorified. – Romans 8:28-30 (NKJV)

There is nothing that Zariyah can ever do to change my thoughts toward her. Despite her flaws, the attitudes or tantrums, ignoring my requests, or annoying habits, I will always see the beauty that I carried within me and birthed to become her. None of that will ever change. The day she comes to realize her worth will be the day that she upgrades her crown from that of a princess to that of a queen. The blessing of motherhood is to see what our parents saw in us. That insight is illuminated when we look at our own children, as we can see more clearly and realize when we take the concept further, why God views us in such a loving way.

⁷ But we have this treasure in earthen vessels, that the excellence of the power may be of God and not of us. (2 Corinthians 4:7 NKJV)

Zariyah's arrival in my life was the first of many landmarks on the road to me discovering my unique power—the power I possessed to become a heroine in my own right. I discovered that I was not chosen to be Zariyah's mother to make her into the perfect daughter or woman. My job was to make her capable—capable of becoming the woman that she was created to be, regardless of what I may desire for her. I am responsible every day for instilling value, worth, courage, and insight into the world that she is a part of. While she is young, my desires outweigh her own. Once she shows signs of having her own ideals and perception of life, my role changes to guide, so I can nurture her in ways that supports her well-being and growth. As she continues to develop, she may even venture down paths completely different from my own. But, my original task set before me to carry out will remain very much intact: to LOVE her.

No matter what she becomes or does in her lifetime, the burden I carry in loving this child will never change. For 37 weeks, she was a part of me and, despite being separated physically from her attachment to my birth canal, traces of her memory will never fade from my being.

In much the same manner, God's message to me (and to all of us) is that no matter where we roam throughout our lives', His presence will always be near us, anticipating any call on Him. Our

Seven — Treasured

memories never fade from Him either. He will never stop loving us, never stop fighting for us behind hidden prayer closets, and never stop urging our progress. Why? Because He knows our worth is beyond anything we can see with our own eyes.

I am worth loving.
I am worth fighting for.
I am worth pursuing and encouraging to keep pushing upwards.
I am so convicted of this that I wish to repeat it:

I am worth loving, I am worth fighting for, and I am worth pursuing and encouraging to keep pushing upwards.

For so many people we find it easy to comprehend these stories of victory for others but draw the line for ourselves, but let me say that this is your right too!!

God used Zariyah to show me how Princesses are born every day, with so much promise and hope tucked into every essence of their tiny beings. Even if our stories never end with us kissing the prince and finding that perfect adaptation of the happily-ever-after ending many of us seek, that does not mean that our titles were ever severed. Your right to claim royalty is very much intact, and now is as good as any time to claim it.

Declaration

I believe and I agree that I was created on purpose for a purpose that can never be taken away. I was chosen from conception because I have a calling unique to any other individual and that is exactly why I exist. I renounce every negative thought, word and action that attempted to stop me from living out my right as a daughter of the Most High God and I ask you Lord for forgiveness for allowing myself and others to distract me from hearing You. Please draw me under the shadow of your wings as scripture states,

[1] *Whoever dwells in the shelter of the Most High*
will rest in the shadow of the Almighty.
[2] *I will say of the Lord, "He is my refuge and my fortress,*
my God, in whom I trust."

³ Surely he will save you

from the fowler's snare

and from the deadly pestilence.

⁴ He will cover you with his feathers,

and under his wings you will find refuge;

his faithfulness will be your shield and rampart.

⁵ You will not fear the terror of night,

nor the arrow that flies by day,

⁶ nor the pestilence that stalks in the darkness,

nor the plague that destroys at midday.

⁷ A thousand may fall at your side,

ten thousand at your right hand,

but it will not come near you.

⁸ You will only observe with your eyes

and see the punishment of the wicked.

⁹ If you say, "The Lord is my refuge,"

and you make the Most High your dwelling,

¹⁰ no harm will overtake you,

no disaster will come near your tent.

¹¹ For he will command his angels concerning you

to guard you in all your ways;

¹² they will lift you up in their hands,

Declaration

so that you will not strike your foot against a stone.

¹³ You will tread on the lion and the cobra;

you will trample the great lion and the serpent.

¹⁴ "Because he loves me," says the Lord, "I will rescue him;

I will protect him, for he acknowledges my name.

¹⁵ He will call on me, and I will answer him;

I will be with him in trouble,

I will deliver him and honor him.

¹⁶ With long life I will satisfy him

and show him my salvation." (Psalm 91:1-16 NIV)

If you have never accepted the Lord as your Saviour and want to, but don't know how, I invite you to repeat this prayer:

> *Lord God of Abraham, Isaac and Jacob (Israel),*
> *I come before you, humbly—acknowledging my faults and all the shortcomings that separate me from having a relationship with you. I truly desire to repent and turn away from all my wrongdoing. Though I cannot be perfect, I thank You for sending your Son Jesus (Yeshua) who—through His sacrificial death—made it possible to restore me to a place of acceptance. I ask you to be the Lord of my life and to help me*

on this journey as I seek to follow you as best as I can, in Your Name I pray, Amen.

Congratuations!

If you've committed your life to God, I would love to hear from you so I can pray for you and send resources to help you on your way.

Email me at **hello@dashoffinesse.com**

Thoughts – Notes – Doodles

www.ingramcontent.com/pod-product-compliance
Lightning Source LLC
Chambersburg PA
CBHW040107120526
44589CB00039B/2769